MINE

by
Bil Keane

FAWCETT GOLD MEDAL • NEW YORK

"SCHOOL'S OUT!"

"Sum-mertime -- and the livin' is easy..."

"No, we're not doing anything BAD...but, it's not GOOD either. It's sort of in-between."

"Stand right there, Daddy, and I'll swim all the way over to you."

"Are you playing singles, Mommy, or are we all
going to play mixed-up doubles?"

"That tomato isn't
ripe yet."   "I'll put it back."

"Is it okay if I take a bath now?"

"It's stopped raining. Can we go out and see if
there's a RAINBOAT in the sky?"

"I almost caught the ball today, but it got to me before I could get my hands out of my pockets."

"I'm hot, Mommy, will you turn on the windmill?"

"I'll be camping out back till dinnertime."

"Stop treading on PJ, Jeffy!" "I'm tellin' on
YOU, Dolly!" "Quit it, Billy!"
"MOMMY!"

"I hope they don't all reach the bottom at the same time."

"I wish you'd buy us a swing like THEIRS!"

"Get down lower, Daddy—I can't pitch that high."

"Poor Daddy. He's so happy when he's leaving to play tennis. but he always comes home lookin' mad."

"Aren't you coming in, too, Mommy?"

"Can't we leave for the drive-in movie NOW, Daddy? We could play on the swings till it starts."

"Go 'way, Kittycat! YOU'RE no rabbit!"

"Jeffy's p'lutin'!"

"The telephone was ringing, but I made it stop."

"Daddy showed me how we're going to get to the ocean from here and it's only THIS FAR!"

"We better take my rock collection with us in case
some burglars get in while we're away."

"I don't know which is longer—the night before Christmas or the night before vacation."

"This is the worst part about goin'
on vacation."

"It's 10:30, Daddy—I thought you said
we were going to leave at 8."

"Can Dolly ride up front with you?
She might get car sick."

"According to this map, the next state we go into will
be all PURPLE."

"Aw, Daddy! That's the fourth town we've gone through without seeing a good place to stop for lunch. We're HUNGRY!"

"There goes the truck we passed this morning, and
there's the trailer we passed,
and there goes ..."

"Jeffy keeps waving to the people behind us and they're STRANGERS!"

"Couldn't we go down to the beach first and unpack
all our junk later?"

"Hi! We're movin' in right above you!"

"We've been walking on the beach, collecting shells
and watching the gulls and everything, Mommy!
You're missing the whole vacation!"

"We're going to the BEACH!"

"Mommy! Daddy! Watch
me! Look what I can
do! Ya watchin'?"

"Blow on it, Mommy! Blow on it!"

"Wow! This is great! We really NEED this! First steady
rain we've had in weeks!"

"...Continued fair and warm throughout the Mid-
west, sunny and hot in the Southwest, fine summer
weather in the New England states ..."

"What happened to the castle we built
here yesterday?"

"Go stand some place else, Jeffy!
You're ruining my suntan!"

"Why does God keep flushing the ocean?"

"Billy had a bite of candy, so he can't go into the
water for an hour—right, Mommy?"

"Which card shall I send to Grandma—the one with moonlight on the water or the one with the lady on the beach?"

"Mommy, why does this 'nilla ice cream
taste so crunchy?"

"I'm tellin' Barfy and Sam when we get home!
You guys were petting another dog!"

"... And four hamburgers."

"We'd . . . better start . . . jogging back . . .
before you guys . . . get too . . . tired."

"Don't buy anything at the store for tonight, Mommy!
We're gonna CATCH our dinner!"

"Daddy, make those dumb ol' fishies stop eating the
bait off my hook!"

"Daddy, couldn't you phone your boss and ask for one more week off?"

"I was just down saying 'goodby to the ocean an'
this BIG wave came along . . ."

"When does somebody else get to lie on the bag of
dirty laundry?"

• "Two ice teas, four milks and a knife to cut the cakes
they brought in with them."

". . And we swam in the ocean, and played on the beach, and we fished and went to the 'musement park and LOTSA stuff! How was YOUR vacation?"

"Mommy! NOW how many days till Billy gets back to school?"

"Aren't we gonna DO anything for Labor Day?"

"And there's STILL enough sand in the car to fill their sandbox!"

"ANYWAY, while you're at school we're gonna watch 'Captain Kangaroo' and 'Hollywood Squares' and 'Sesame Street' and 'Let's Make A Deal', and . . ."

•"I CAN'T carry them to school for Miss Lee
cause I might have to scratch my nose or
tie my shoe or pat a dog or..."

"Daddy! Do I have to go to bed now?"

"I like those oranges that are easy to unzip best.
The ones called tambourines."

"The difference between dogs and cats is cats
like to THINK about what they're
going to do."

"I have a big tummy so I get THREE cookies,
your tummy is littler so you get TWO..."

"When Mommy had the bottom off the toaster I got to look in and see the engine."

"My cupcake ran out of icing. Can it
have more?"

"GIDEE-UP! GIDEE-UP!"

"Dolly takes her dolls to bed -- why can't I
take my trucks?"

"Grandma, can I borrow a bite of your cake?"

"You don't have to look, Daddy--I'M looking."

"Mommy made a cake and cookies, too, and
didn't holler at us once today, and let us
watch TV...I bet she and Daddy are
going out tonight!"

"Mrs. Delporte says we should get Kittycat a spade so she won't be havin' a lot of kittens."

"If you cry, Mommy will give you a cookie and that'll make it better."

"I know it's Phoenix, Arizona and Detroit, Michigan, but what's Omaha's last name?"

"Mommy, were the ghosts you and Daddy were
watching on TV real or not?"

"I can hold my OWN
hand crossing the
street!"

"There's nothing to do over at Melanie's house.
Their TV set had to go to the shop."

"I'm full of aches and pains from this cold, but
what hurts most are my fingers from
coloring so much."

"Daddy blew me a kiss but I didn't catch it!"

"Here he is, Mommy. He's not into anything yet, but stand by for a late bulletin!"

"Miss Lee is gettin' married and we have to learn
to spell her new name. It's Mihaleckovich!"

"Member when Sam was a little pup and we used
to put newspapers on the kitchen floor for
him to read?"

"Aw, Mommy! I'll be goin' back out again in a few minutes."

"Why do some of our cousins have the same last name as us and some don't?"

"Could I have a note for the bus driver saying it's okay for me and Greg to play football on the bus?"

"Boy, Dolly! If there's one thing you can't do, it's
POUR!"

"Miss Elaine is a GOOD teacher—she lets us climb on the desks."

"We had art today. Did you know Van Gogh cut off
his ear?"

"What should I dream about tonight?"

"How can their shoes wear out so fast when we DRIVE them every place they go?"

"Listen, Mommy! The boys stopped fighting!
Should I go see what they're into?"

"This letter from Grandma is real fat. Bet she
cut some more cartoons out of the paper
'cause they 'minded her of us!"

"Boy! Is kittycat mad! She's been locked in the closet all night!"

"You said I'd have a BLACK eye, but it's PURPLE."

"I can tell which is my right hand and which is my left even with my eyes CLOSED!"

"Who do you hope wins, Daddy?"

"Don't hot it, Mommy!"

"I know your maiden name was Thelma Carne, but what was DADDY'S maiden name?"

"Mommy just washed my hair and Jeffy touched
it with his dirty hands."

"I don't know my address but the zip code
is 85253."

"Shh! Mommy's talking to Grandma and she's sick in bed! Do you want to make her worse?"

"Why can't I get my nurse's kit and go with you
to help take care of Grandma?"

"Wave your whole arm, Jeffy. You can't 'spect
Mommy to see you opening and closing
your fingers."

"Now Daddy is in full charge and we have to listen to him just like he was Mommy!"

"...And the first one who says 'that's not how
Mommy does it' is in real trouble!"

"That's not the way Mommy cooks my...I mean,
boy oh, boy! That egg looks VERY good!"

"Aw, Daddy -- when Mommy calls us in the
morning she doesn't yell 'up and at 'em!'"

"When Grandma comes out of the hospital, maybe she'll bring a baby like Mrs. Dean did."

"Want a baloney sandwich, or a couple of peanut
butter and jelly sandwiches? Or some cup-
cakes? Cookies? My father packed
my lunch."

"Mommy always puts a NAPKIN in my lunch."

"Tonight it's going to be MY turn to sleep in Mommy's place!"

"Thanks, Elaine, but we're having dinner tonight at Tina's, and tomorrow at Peterson's. Let's see, we could fit you in Monday or Tuesday."

"Billy's blue pants are in his middle drawer...
Dolly's green jumper is on a hanger in the
utility room...Hurry! The bus will be
there in five minutes!"

"G'NIGHT, MOMMY!"

"Daddy's cookin' is SUPER, Mommy! We have
had chicken, pizza, hamburgers, and tonight
we're havin' CHINESE food!"

"I made this for Grandma, Daddy. Will you put it in an envelope and mail it? But, don't fold it."

"It's okay, Kathy, get in! My Daddy's almost
as good a driver as Mommy."

"Well, Daddy, how do you like bein'
a BACHELOR?"

"I'm glad you're feeling better, Grandma...No, this is DOLLY -- that was BILLY you just talked to...I think Jeffy wants to say hello now..."

"Hurry, Daddy! Jack LaLanne's on! Time for our exercises!"

"Understand, honey? Mommy won't be
home tomorrow -- she'll be here the
NEXT tomorrow."

"Should we take Mommy's plants to a doctor
before she gets home?"

"I almost forgot what you look like, Mommy,
but NOW I 'member!"

"...And we vacuumed and dusted, and put out the trash and we EVEN MADE THE BEDS!"

"Careful, Mommy—don't wipe that smile
off his face."

You can have lots more fun
with
BIL KEANE and
THE FAMILY CIRCUS

30   Allow at least 4 weeks for delivery.   TA-60